My Pet Memory Book

About This Book

This book is designed to help children who have lost a pet. The book allows them to fill in all the information they like about their pet, and has plenty of room for pictures- either drawn or to stick in photographs. Parents can help the child fill the book in if needed.

Children can fill in as much or as little of the book as they like, and at their own pace. Using the book will help them as they grieve for their lost pet by helping them recall memories which they can record. They will be able to look at the book whenever they like in the future which makes it a lovely keepsake, and also reassures the child that the pet will never be forgotten.

About The Author

This book was created to help the Author's children when one of the family pets sadly died. The children were worried that they would forget their pet. The book meant that they could record their memories of the pet so that he wouldn't be forgotten, and helped the children remember their happiest memories of him.

The Author also works in Education and writes children's story books.

ISBN: 9781793164995

About My Pet

My Pet's Name _____

Breed _____

Age _____

About Me

My Name _____

Age _____

Where I Live _____

My Family _____

Me and My Pet

My Pet and Our Family

My Pet's Favourite Things To Do

My Pet's Favourite Places To Go

My Pet's Favourite Food and Treats

My Pet's Favourite Toys

My Pet's Favourite Place To Sleep

My Pet's Favourite Things To Do With Me

My Favourite Things to Do With My Pet

The Silliest Things My Pet Did

The Funniest Things My Pet Did

The Naughtiest Things My Pet Did

What Other People Loved About My Pet

My Pet's Favourite People

My Pet's Favourite Animals

My Favourite Memories About My Pet

What My Pet Loved About Me

What I Loved About My Pet

Why My Pet Wouldn't Want Me To Be Sad

_____

_____

_____

_____

_____

_____

_____

_____

_____

_____

_____

_____

_____

_____

_____

_____

What Reminds Me of My Pet
(So I'll Never Forget Them)

_____

_____

_____

_____

_____

_____

_____

_____

_____

_____

_____

_____

_____

_____

_____

_____

_____

Use this space to write anything you like about your pet-
their birthday, when they came to live with you, where they
came from, how you chose them etc.

Made in the USA
Middletown, DE
06 February 2024

49206901R00029